BOLT

Acknowledgments

These poems have previously manifested in various forms, including publications, sound scores, performances, recordings, films, and dance collaborations. They have been sung and spoken, in singular and multiple voices, alternating and simultaneous. Some are new, and some have been bobbing and weaving in and out of my psyche for 30 years. Many thanks to the teachers and collaborators I've had the pleasure to work with, to the people, real and imagined, who have wound their way into the poems, and to Anvil Press for taming these pieces into a single volume.

Some poems in this collection originally appeared in *The Capilano Review, Quills, ribsauce: a cd/anthology of words by women* edited by Alex Boutros, Kaarla Sundström and Taien Ng-Chan, and *Fresh Tracks: Writing The Western Landscape* edited by Pamela Banting.

BOLT

Hilary Peach

ANVIL PRESS • CANADA

Copyright © 2018 by Hilary Peach

Anvil Press Publishers Inc.
P.O. Box 3008, Main Post Office
Vancouver, B.C. V6B 3X5 CANADA
www.anvilpress.com

All rights reserved. No part of this book may be reproduced by any means without the prior written permission of the publisher, with the exception of brief passages in reviews. Any request for photocopying or other reprographic copying of any part of this book must be directed in writing to Access Copyright: The Canadian Copyright Licensing Agency, One Yonge Street, Suite 800, Toronto, Ontario, Canada, M5E 1E5.

Library and Archives Canada Cataloguing in Publication

Peach, Hilary, author
    Bolt / Hilary Peach. — First edition.

Poems.
ISBN 978-1-77214-116-0 (softcover)

    I. Title.

PS8631.E218B65 2018   C811'.6   C2018-901889-5

Printed and bound in Canada
Cover design by Rayola Graphic Design
Interior by HeimatHouse
Represented in Canada by Publishers Group Canada
Distributed by Raincoast Books

The publisher gratefully acknowledges the financial assistance of the Canada Council for the Arts, the Government of Canada, and the Province of BritishColumbia through the B.C. Arts Council and the Book Publishing Tax Credit.

bolt¹ |b lt|
1. (noun) a threaded pin used to fasten things together.
2. (noun) a flash of lightning, leaving a jagged line across the sky.
3. (verb) to run away, suddenly out of control, as a horse.

table of contents

1. **Blackbirds Hold the Souls**
    Wallflowers   11
    Tattoo   12
    This Is the Picture to Be Repeated   13
    Love Is a Small Town   17
    Loretta   21
    Don't Go Outside   23
    Making Up the Weather   26
    At the Feeder   31
    Blackbirds Hold the Souls of Those In Purgatory   32
    A Dream Deferred (The Economizer Song)   39
    Appaloosa   41
    The Anvils Are Restless   46

2. **Rhapsody of Scars**
    The Great Cathedral   51
    Montana   56
    Michigan   67
    Pennsylvania   70
    Judy, I Remembered   77
    The Mouse   81

3. Dictionary of Snakes
    You Are Camping   89
    Oh, My Dear   92
    The Letter   95
    Esmeralda   98

4. These Tangled Mustangs
    The Last Frontier   103
    Miles City   105
    Cowboys Dream   107
    Buffalo   113
    Outlaw Girls   115

BLACKBIRDS
HOLD THE
SOULS

Wallflowers

wallflowers
are fabulous dancers
the girls whose summer nights
are steeped in grief
that's how they find
their secret pleasures
naked in the heartland
sideswiping the rooms
of empty, dreamlike houses
with their beautiful moves

Tattoo

he said I bought this cross
on the island of St. Thomas
because I wanted Jesus on my chest

and I got this tattoo down in New Orleans,
this one in Reno, on my honeymoon
when I married my first wife
for the second time

I got this scar
the night I rolled the Bronco
I bought this heart
out of the back of a magazine

I know it's ripped
but it came like this,
it came like this

I got these stories
in a kind of pawnshop
along with this leather coat
and this gold wristwatch

and I picked you up
on the side of the road
and I'd have taken you home
but my hands were broken

This Is the Picture to Be Repeated

I was walking
I was walking today
I was walking today when suddenly
I was reminded of you

This is the picture:
a woman stands at a sink
washing her hands
one then the other

I was walking
I was walking today when suddenly
I saw something
and it reminded me of you

This is the picture:
a woman stands erect at a sink
washing one arm
then the other

I saw something
I saw something today
while I was walking
something which reminded me of you

This is the picture:
a woman stands naked at a basin
scrubbing herself methodically
with a coarse cloth

I was walking today when
suddenly I saw something
I saw something falling
and it reminded me of you

A woman stands naked at a basin
in front of a window
scrubbing herself methodically
with a coarse cloth

I saw a woman today
while I was falling
methodically a woman
and she reminded me of you

This picture will be repeated:
a woman stands in front of a mirror
pouring hot water
into a basin

I saw a woman
and she reminded me of you
falling one way and then the other
over and over

This is the picture:
a woman stands at a sink
washing herself methodically
one hand then the other

over and over
as she has always
been washing herself
she has always been doing that

I saw you today
it reminded me of you
it reminded me of falling
over and over

one way and then the other
as you have always
been falling
you have always been doing that

A woman stands in front of a mirror
by a window naked and erect
as always and washes over and
over one arm and then the other

I saw you today
while I was walking
I saw you and suddenly
I was reminded of this woman:

she's walking and it's raining
and she starts washing herself
suddenly over and over
one hand and then the other

She has always been doing that
rain has always been falling
one way or another
over and over

I saw you today
while I was walking
I saw you today
and suddenly you started raining

suddenly you started raining
you were pouring
like a woman pouring hot water
into a basin

it reminded me of you
you have always been falling
one way or another
you have always been doing that

I was washing today
when suddenly I saw you
walking into a woman
and it reminded me of something

it reminded me of you
falling into a woman
over and over like a coarse cloth
you have always been falling

this is the picture to be repeated

Love Is a Small Town

you always said that I was right
that I was too kind
I said that you were rigorous
undisciplined
and I wanted to learn how to swim

hey-hey you can swim now you can
learn how to dive
hey-hey you can dive now you can
learn how to sleep soundly

hey you can learn to take me in your stride

love
is a small town
where everyone knows what's going down
where everyone shows her own small soul
in the hardware store at the end of the road

love
is a supermarket
where all the aisles are named
after local streets
and the produce section is where you meet
your old girlfriends

and love
is a barroom brawl
with the waitress calling

break it up   break it up
break it up   you two
take it outside   give me your keys
you're both   too drunk to drive

and love is a gas station
with an empty shop
and all the machines have been
locked out
and turned off

you can telephone
but I won't see you
you're on your own now
and I dream

to the ceiling
out the open window
and your eyes
still send me reeling
they won't stop revealing
all your open skies

they're still part of your disguise

I remember when the doctors told me
that you were old and tired
and I didn't believe them
I didn't believe what I could see

and I remember when the undertaker came calling

I asked him   *just what is it*
                that you intend to take under?

and he said your mouth
                was like a dream

I remember when
the photographer came
and she said
      this is news
      this is really news
      this is really big news
      there's no news like news
      there's no news like big news
      like real news
      like really new news

and all the neighbours
were crowding into the living room
and they were whispering to each other

how could this happen?
how could this happen?

there were a lot of strangers
gathering out on the front lawn
and they were shouting at each other

what happened?
what happened?

there's been an accident
a terrible accident
there's been a train crash

somebody forgot to throw the switch
somebody forgot to change the track
just when you were looking forward
you started to roll back
now you're caught in your tracks

and it's rolling
it's a wild ride
it's a sing-song sing-song
it's been a long time
it's history
it's an old bone
it's your mouth
saying I'm coming home

it's your mouth
saying I'm coming home

Loretta

Loretta
don't you tell those boys
where we've been
the weather
over the mountain
signifies change
you are as wet as the rain

I fell in love with a girl
when I was twenty one
but she never said
that we were together
she was married
she called him her old man

I would tease her
when she sneaked out at night to meet me
I said I must be your old woman

we used to sit in the tall grass
at the edge of the world
and share a secret between us
and sometimes we'd steal horses
and ride them along those
long dry country roads

Loretta
don't you tell those boys where we've been
the weather over the mountain

signifies change
you are as wet as the rain
you are as cold
as an evening's resolution

you woke up this morning
with a halo wrapped around your head
I took it as a warning
of something old and strange
these winds are changing
direction and getting colder

this old man he played once
he left her because he wanted too much
he met me in a mysterious restaurant
I had no idea I had no idea I said
what do you want?

Loretta
don't you tell
those boys
where we've been
I thought
you'd have forgiven me
we come from
different directions
these winds
                    are changing us

Don't Go Outside

don't go outside
it is too apocalyptic
the fogthick smoke
from someone else's wildfire
enshrouding your everything

don't go on social media
where your everyone
is panicky and yacking
assing up the airwaves
with their sass talk
of evacuation

do go to the suddenly called
emergency preparedness meeting
where the hysteria mixes with
solid information like
a strong drink

in the event of an emergency we
will all go to the community hall
and each be assigned an
8' x 10' taped-off area
on the floor
where we can sleep
for the next 72 hours

Will there be conjugal taped-off areas?
Bruce asked

you know, like, if you want to get it on?
Bruce and his girl do not see themselves
sleeping in a taped-off area
and neither do I
better the unburning forest
or a beach or
                sandspit

it was strongly suggested we each pack
a grab-'n'-go bag and leave it
by the front door
and I will do it
even with that clumsy double contraction
and dutifully include
my passport ID spare keys
jewelry and a substantial amount of money

and if I were I thief
I would drive around and reach inside
the many unlocked houses
into the hallways
where people were told to place
these bags of irreplaceables and cash
and I would take them

you could say
I'd be grabbin'-'n'-goin'

don't forget to include a
flashlight and fresh water
the VHF handheld radio
in case anyone is listening

smoked oysters maybe and antipasto
artisan fig crackers
pre-almond-shaming almonds
the scotch
dijon, chocolate
some good reading
the rest can be replaced

to the fire gods I consign
the bill bissets and
the Gibson Girl print
the 1929 L-1
and that nice cutting board
just like the one on Masterchef

Send a copy of the emergency plan
to someone I love?
                          OK — here it is
    grab the bag of snacks
    grab the ones you love
    get in the boat
    and go

If you need us
we'll be on the water
watching it all   go up in smoke

Making Up the Weather
for Pat Morford

all over this island
people wake up and think it's you
smashing the clouds together
breaking thunder
                        playing
with your favourite things
and changing the weather
but this seems
so far fetched
we all know that
it is really Zeus
conducting the reformation
of molecules

whoever it is
is having a good time
it feels like dangerous play
the way the ground shakes
the house shudders

            the flashes so young
            so bright and fast
            so brilliant

like meaning or a better word
on the periphery
that you can't quite
get a hold of

in the morning
everyone is talking about it
and saying nothing
the chatter never stops
meanwhile the birds have shut right up
or they are just more cautious
and there are fewer of them

in an interview Neil Young said
    I don't choose the people in my band
    because of the instruments they play
    I choose people who like to chase an idea
    around a room
    it's like you're making up the weather

Zeus has been making
more coal-fired electric plants in China
around two hundred this year
their carbon emissions
roughly equivalent to the annual
energy output of Brazil

the media is flooded
with nonsensical comparisons
560 million tonnes
of information per year
roughly equivalent to
the total biomass of ants
in the tropical rainforest,
and coal consumption
is now measured

in premature deaths
>	*we were all so sorry*
>	*to see you go*
>	*so young*
>	*so bright and fast*
>	*so brilliant*

meanwhile we have been told
we will start taking apart
the coal plants in Alberta
in seven years
well, six now, maybe five

this I understand
the slow disassembly of a boiler
cutting apart the wall-tube panels
dismantling the superheaters
a turbine blade's beautiful descent
from the end of a jib

I will probably go
and every day we will drive
through prairie weather
to get there
through birdsong and thunder
through the ice storms that feel
like you are driving right into
a porcupine's ass

I saw my first porcupine
in Montana

tall as the side mirror on a Chevy Nova
spiny as a pricklypear cactus
round as a tumbleweed

at the coal plant there
they warned us about fugitive dust
and rogue gas
as though the pollutants
had just escaped from custody
tiny carcinogens in prison garb
lurking in the parking lot
ready to jack your ride

wherever there are power plants
there are ospreys nesting
in the transmission towers
occasionally one of these
is struck by lightning
then the plant is closed
and the ground is dusted lightly
with feathers

you are the bravest person I know
and I keep forgetting to tell you
when you are dead
when you are alive
when you are dead
when you are alive
all of you

you have been so kind to me

and I keep forgetting to thank you
when you are dead
when you are alive
when you are missing
when you are right here

hanging in my eyes
like a beautiful storm
like a charm
like a love letter
like a long drive
like an osprey
like a song
>	*so young*
>	*so bright and fast*
>	*so brilliant*

when you are here
when you are dead
when you are alive
when you are making up
the weather

At the Feeder

there are two kinds of nuthatches and someone very red
and someone very yellow, chickadee dee dee and someone
very large who casts a wide shadow and causes some of them
to shriek and some to go silent, and some come in pairs and
some come in groups of five, and Mr. Upsidedown always
comes alone, spinning like an acrobat, one foot flexing open
and closed, talking to the sky, the other gripping a twig,
turning, beak to the earth, amen

and Squirrel Monday barks and chips but it is not him because
he is too guttural and his head is enormous and his eyes are clear
and his coat is new and his tail is fine, this is Baby Monday,
fresh and easily frightened with great ear tufts and madly beating
heart, taking his first strides and leaps, testing speed and balance,
feeling cheeky, taking risks, seeing everything, witnessing the
great opening before it begins to unravel

and there upon the earth is someone very scaly and someone
very long, and someone with four toes who lives under the
large boulder and someone who causes the grass to tremble
while he slides between the stalks, and here is someone meek
and big-eared headed for the feeder, and little long-snout scuttling
across the path, the image of the great blue cat emblazoned
forever on the backs of his eyes

Blackbirds Hold the Souls of Those in Purgatory
(score for voice and toy piano)

i.
portrait
portrait of someone
who is having trouble
with belief

when are you
when are you
blue

are you superstitious?

a dog eating grass means rain
a bat flying close
means you will soon be betrayed

they used to say
keep your money in a weasel-skin purse
and you will always have financial security

today they say to keep it in an RRSP
a GIC, hedge funds
you decide
which is better
a weasel-skin purse
or General Motors?

an eagle sitting motionless means an enemy is approaching

meeting a dog is good luck, especially a dalmatian
the gaze of a wolf causes blindness
if a girl walks through a swarm of bees without getting stung
it is a sure sign that she is a virgin

Aspirin stops heart attacks
blueberries prevent cancer
plucking three hairs from a donkey's shoulder
and wearing them in a muslin bag
around the neck will cure measles

have your children vaccinated
don't have your children vaccinated

the biopharmaceutical giant, Pfizar
has just created a drug
that will dramatically reduce the symptoms
of people suffering
from the irrational distrust
of biopharmaceutical companies

sitting backwards
on a donkey
is a cure for snakebite

ii.

when are you
when you
are blue

here
in this room
on this ocean

this is the day we remember a friend
whose ashes we poured
into the arms of the sea

and he surprised us
by becoming a radiant green cloud
and hundreds of small, clear jellyfish
swam in the same direction
through what once
was his body

if you count the number of fish you've caught
you will catch no more that day
meeting a goat on an important journey
means good luck
it is bad luck to say the word *pig*
while fishing at sea

pig
pig

iii.
in the dream
a monkey
swung from a branch
in the tree outside
outside my window

he swung onto the windowsill
and asked
what makes you happy
and i said
                    happy?
i like to play
and the monkey asked
what do you play
and i said i play
i play a little piano

singing before breakfast brings bad luck
a cat washing behind its ears means rain

wait
start again

iv.
a little talisman
maybe a ring
maybe a pen
a star

she's writing a letter
she's writing a letter to explain
why she no longer bothers
to write letters
she's writing a letter to plumb
her own disbelief
she cannot throw off these answers
they swarm, like bees

bees will deliberately sting the person
who swears in front of them
hiding in a bull's pen
gives you immunity from lightning

a bat flying close to a person
means that person
will soon be betrayed

v.

this was the day
she cursed him
and it worked like a charm
he was an instrument builder
and she was a deckchair

the curse went like this
that something would happen to him
that would keep him
from ever being himself
yet cause him
to always remember

there was a fire
and a fall
and when he woke up
the doctors had sewn
his hand to his chest

someone said   *look what you've done*
and someone else said   *he had it coming*

she felt only relief
knowing he could no longer carve
his initials into her arm

vi.

a rabbit running down a street
means a house will catch fire
cows lying down mean rain
it is bad luck to cross a stream while carrying a cat
for reasons which seem obvious

harming a wren means a broken bone
an owl is the only creature who abides a ghost and
blackbirds hold the souls of those in purgatory

but don't despair　　　　　never despair
if you throw away a dead mouse, the wind
will blow from that direction
bats flying playfully
and dolphins swimming north
mean fine weather
using this hair product will make you look
a little bit more like Angelina Jolie than you do now
subscribing to radical self-love
means you can manifest your destiny
meeting a monkey is good luck
and if you run into a spider's web
you will make a new friend

if you meditate daily
you will be marginally more likely to

have the sweet life you dream of
and get it on with someone beautiful

a swan's feather sewed into a husband's pillow
ensures fidelity
eating the flesh of another person
is really bad
and wearing Celine Dione's perfume
means you will belong

you will no longer be poor
you will no longer be unemployed
you will no longer be sick
you will no longer be homeless
you will no longer feel despair
you will no longer feel the planet warming up

blackbirds hold the souls of those in purgatory
blackbirds hold the souls of those in purgatory
blackbirds hold the souls of those in purgatory until judgement day
blackbirds
hold the souls

when you
when you
are blue

A Dream Deferred (The Economizer Song)

I was watching the view
when I nearly got hit by a train
I was thinking about you
and how I'd probably
never call you again

because you only think about her
she's a dream deferred
and your eyes are over the horizon

you've been with her for years
you asked me why she'd
throw in the towel
there are only so many reasons,
and I'll tell you boy, I know them all

but I wouldn't worry too much about them
she's only dreaming of him
and I'm watching you
while you think about her
she's a dream deferred
and your eyes are over the horizon

the boys in the band
are all your fans
the girls in the stands
have their eyes on you

when you're making amends
to her family and friends
you know they've got no reason
they've got no reason to lie to you

that was all
that was all over
that was all over nothing
that was all over nothing at all
over nothing

now she's got your love
and she's got your money
she's got your love
and she's got your money
she's got your love
and she's got your money
she's got your love
and she's got your money
she's got your love
and she's got your money

that was all
that was all over
that was all over nothing at all
over nothing

Appaloosa

sometimes
sometimes
sometimes
sometimes
sometimes
sometimes
sometimes

you see it coming
sometimes
sometimes
sometimes
sometimes
you want it so bad
sometimes
sometimes
it looks like a trap

sometimes
sometimes
her name is lady luck
and she's audible
she's incorrigible
she's adorable

now she's cold and furious
and you're on that curious appaloosa
the one with the name
that sounds like a drink

and the mane
that is spun from silver
and goodness.

sometimes
sometimes
sometimes
it comes out of the blue

sometimes
sometimes
she's a vixen
a fox you can criss-cross
a rapid you shoot
sometimes
sometimes
her name is lady luck

she's a game you can run
(   )
and she's cold
(   )
and furious
(   )
and you're on that
(   )
curious
(   )
appaloosa
(   )
the one with the name

(   )
that sounds like a drink
(.   )
and a mane that is spun from
silver and goodness

oh those big-boned appaloosas
sometimes
sometimes
all loose-limbed and long-bodied
sometimes
sometimes
you hold your breath
sometimes
sometimes
sometimes
sometimes
he reminds you of somebody
sometimes
sometimes
sometimes
sometimes
you feel like death
sometimes
sometimes

no courage
no pony
how do you know
the enemy?
he said

no courage
no pony

it would
always be wrong
it would always be wrong
it would always be wrong
it would always be wrong

it would always be wrong
it would always be wrong
it would always be wrong

I would always be wrong
I would always be wrong
I would always be wrong

I would always be wrong
I would always be wrong
I would always be wrong again
in all ways be wrong
I would always be wrong again
in all ways be wrong

and now
I am cold and furious
and he's on that curious
appaloosa
the one with the name
that sounds like a drink
and the mane that is spun from

silver and goodness

(sometimes? sometimes.
sometimes? sometimes.)

oh those northern horses
those spotted ghosts

o those
big-boned appaloosas
all tall and loose

all long-bodied
walleyed and thunder
chest-deep in the pond water

they make you want to give it all
for a little wonder

o those big-boned appaloosas
all tall and loose
all long-bodied
walleyed and thunder
chest-deep in the pond
they make you want to give it all
for a little wonder
they make you
give it all

for a little
wonder

The Anvils Are Restless

and ramble out
onto the main road
rumbling the moonlight
their square hooves slow
as handwriting
deliberate as ice

in older times
they roamed more freely
in greater numbers
were less guarded
and so were we
scarred with chiselmarks
scorched with hope

anvils remember everything
every thing that they have
ever made
every blow and ring

and we
will make everything
or we say we will
or we want to
or we want to say
we will
make everything
out of everything
seamless and heavy

tender hammerblows
ringing bright as stone

anvils live for two hundred
or three hundred years
if they live at all
if they aren't captured
during the dark times
confiscated and rendered
into arms

that was a long time ago

tonight
they are skittish
on the move
making a break for it
they angle swaybacked
down the main road
swinging their great horns
from side to side
their breath
cool as smoke
the scent of something
tenderly uncertain
on the air

RHAPSODY
OF SCARS

The Great Cathedral

there is no work in our own
hometowns anymore
because they've moved
the factories away

so we get in our cars
on our big horses
and we ride

we drive and we drive
and we leave our families behind
we live on coffee
and quick meaty truck stop specials
we fall right off the map and onto the next one
as one radio station fades out
another comes in
and our hearts open up
fill with prairie winds

we're called travel cards, permits
transients, boomers
tradesmen and a few women
snaking across the continent
in motor homes and pick-up trucks
rotted out cars
the occasional hot rod

we come from both coasts
from the deep south

drop down over the border from Canada
into the pocket of America
to worship at the last
of the great cathedrals
                the power plants
                  of American Electric

they turn coal into current
punch holes in the sky
create their own clouds
but there are no angels on them
no cherubic influences at all

just the waitress, after work
who will cash your paycheque
bring you a beer
a cheese steak sandwich
and an envelope of hundreds
on a lonely Saturday night

oh boy
here we go again
another spring
just like clockwork
as sure as the geese are flying home
we head south, east, north, west
following the rumours
that will lead us to gold

we come
like flies
like fish
like flowers
like seeds
like trains
like birds
like dogs
like rivers

towards the job
towards the job
into the sweet music

and the women
the women who do it
must be making
some sort of special statement
to spend their days
face down in the mud-drum
their nights in that shabby room

ask her
ask her and she'll tell you
all about those female politics
ask her why
and she'll tell you

I'm in it for the music
the money, the sweet long green

she'll say motorcycle
mortgage
summer cabin
summer off
vacation
university
new cello
new windows
new haircut

she's in it to float the boat
to build the bridge
to feed the baby
to buy a new pair of shoes

just like you
just like you

they can't train us fast enough
our numbers are dropping
like flies
like leaves
as the chemicals take us
into the long summer
into the cool river

short lives
long fights
for the widow's pension

but still we go like water
like seeds
like bees to the hive

roll down your window
see those stacks
spires against the cool sky
a parking lot spectral
with fugitive dust
and rogue gas
license plates from Canada
and thirty states

we've come
we've come to lay ourselves down
upon the altar of the god of light
in the last of the great cathedrals

Montana

i.

to get to the job in Montana from where I live
you have to take two ferries and four airplanes
I was searched four times
with metal detectors,
had to empty my pockets, hand luggage
take off my shoes, my belt

everything out of the suitcase
notebook, underwear, brassieres
medicine, playing cards

the trip took two days
filled three credit cards

the last leg was from Forsythe to Colstrip, Montana
150 miles through scrubby tumbleweeds
and cottonwoods, and the only way to get there
was by taxi

home

is the Super 8 Motel
in Colstrip Montana
a woman called Lenora
handing me coffee in
a styrofoam cup

she said   *get ready now*
you're on nightshift
you only got half an hour

it's the kind of town where the hotel desk clerk
will drive you to work

and when we got to the gate
at the Montana Power Plant
a security guard stopped us and asked
if we had any drugs, alcohol, or firearms

Lenora said   *sure Bill, what do you need?*

ii.
inside
I sit down with a newspaper and
sixty gritty American boilermakers
with handlebar moustaches
and divorces hanging
from their belts like scalps.

scars

scars from bottle fights
gunshot wounds,
stabbings and car crashes
scars from barroom brawls
from laying out their motorcycles
and making love

because this is America
home of the brave
land of the free
where there is no Medicare
so you heal rough
because you can't afford the stitches

there is no dental subsidy
so your teeth stay missing

and there is no federally funded technical college
where you can earn your journeyman papers
but there is a lot of prison here
so you pick up your trade in the joint
with four letter words inked
onto your knuckles
or through a labour retraining plan
when you are nearly fifty
because you've poisoned yourself for eighteen years
in the Anaconda copper smelter
and now it's shut down
and they've cancelled your pension

everyone is talking
and no-one is talking to me
I feel like a rabbit
in a coyote colony

after a four-hour safety orientation
three-hour super-heavy-wall tube welding test
criminal record check

immigration confirmation
social security card application
submission of a urine sample
for the purposes of testing for drugs and alcohol
I begin employment

      home of the brave
                land of the free

fifteen of us fit in the freight elevator
it is crowded but there is
a strange halo of space
around me and
I feel like an elk
surrounded by hunters
all trying to get close
but not too close
as though there are antlers
growing out of every part of my body
and I might charge
                I might charge

iii.

in two days I lose
my hotel room because everything
has been booked in advance
Lenora hooks me up
with Doreen, who
is subsidizing her bible franchise
by renting out her
adolescent daughter's room

this town
                    has a grocery store
and a gas station with a small casino in it
it has a Harley shop, a park
and a laundromat with
small casino in it

I meet her at the only restaurant in town
in a bowling alley called the Coal-Bowl
and load my suitcase in with the bibles

iv.

home is a nondescript yellow
vinyl-sided rancher
seventeen miles outside of town
on the side of the highway
there is a pile of dirt in the driveway
and an American flag taped to the window

      home of the brave

the walls are covered in photographs
and dead animal heads
the photographs depict
the son who is in jail
her daughter in a short skirt
standing outside a movie theatre
under a sign that says xxx

hot
       hot
              hot

the animal heads have glassy brown eyes
that follow me from room to room

the photograph of the husband
shows a wild-eyed psychotic
with a shotgun
and a brace of ducks

she tells me he's coming home
released from the detox tomorrow
but she is going to stay with her mother

hmmmm…

land of the free

it was then that I asked
about the axe-shaped splintered holes
in the door to my bedroom
she told me a story
about her daughter
having a temper tantrum and
destroying her room

it seemed reasonable
under the circumstances

after she was gone I noticed
that the holes were larger
on the outside of the door
than the inside
they were made by someone

on the outside of the door,
on the outside,
trying to get in

                with an axe

at work that night
one of the fellas asked me

So, how are you getting along?

        fine, I'm just fine

and then I said

                well, I'll tell you

I've moved to a house
a day's walk from nowhere

the owner is away
she thinks everything that happens to her is a postcard from Jesus
her daughter is making dirty movies in California, her son is in prison
her husband is a compulsive gambler, psychotic, alcoholic gun nut and hunter
he's coming out of the dry-out tomorrow
so we'll be roommates
and there are axe holes the size of my head in the bedroom door

what do you think?
and my colleague said

I think it's time to get out of Dodge
I could pick you up tomorrow, around two?

and I thought
hmmmm

feminist principle...axe murderer
feminist principle...axe murderer

yes, that'll be fine, two o'clock will be just fine

v.

home is an apartment
with the vinyl siding stripped off
by freak hailstorms
I bought a card table and two lawn chairs
at a thrift store, did some laundry
blew five bucks gambling
picked up a fifth of whisky at the gas station
things were getting better

for a month I worked nightshift
welding tubes
on one side of me was a Texan Mexican American
called Javier Gonzales from San Antonio
he had a gold front tooth
and made scorpions out of mechanics' wire

on the other side was a guy called Buddy
he had nine children, and
told me how

for his honeymoon
he took his wife
into the swampland
and they cooked alligator on a spit

                        all night

it was hot

we'd change out of our shirts
hang them off the steel catwalks
seven storeys up
to dry in the desert wind
while the buffaloes
came in to drink
from the reservoir ponds

                        there was no other water

at dinner break
I sat with two guys from the Navajo nation
who fed me animal jerky
but wouldn't tell me what kind of animal it was
when I asked they'd say *coyote* or *prairie dog*

and laugh

                heh heh heh

       making noise
making smoke
all night

vi.

at dawn we went back to the apartments to sleep
and in the afternoons we played
                              basketball
gradually
between the basketball
and the animal jerky
I became so dehydrated I couldn't cry

I filled my empty apartment
with tumbleweeds
because I couldn't believe them
I put one in a box
and mailed it to the arctic
with a tag that said

Instructions:
take to tundra
release

there was a bull snake
about five feet long
dead on the road
outside my apartment
every day
I'd say the words as I stepped over it

                      bull snake
and gradually it became less
and less alarming to see
and gradually the snake dried up
and blew away

slowly losing meaning
until all I was left with
was a piece of its skin
in my pocket
a bare road
and the words.

bull snake
tumbleweeds
animal jerky
alligator spit
reservoir ponds
tundra
buffalo

Michigan
(score for voice and image)

Jesus never lived in Michigan
if he had
he'd have spent his time
fishing
he might have joined the militia
and traded me a pocket knife
at coffee time

Jesus
never worked the power plants
he never drove a Cadillac from state to state
with a suitcase in the back
and a missing plate
these were the thoughts he had
just before he slept
these were thoughts he had
and Blue wept
at the sound of his own heart
missing a beat

Blue wept in a big way
stuck in traffic
behind a coal train
he had a road stake
and a hand-drawn map
and fifty grand left in his old boots
oh he had fifty grand left

and the snow
comes down
in Michigan
and I don't know
when I'm going to see you again
and I think of the dog
in the passenger's seat
and I think of my mom

Blue slept
his whole day away
in the arms of a waitress
with a sweet name
he had a travel card
and some secrets
and a hole the size of a paycheque
in his pocket

how the snow
comes down
in Michigan
and I don't know
when I'm going to see you again
and I think of the dog
in the passenger's seat
and I think of my mom

Cadillac take me
to the old hotel
a man's boots on the stairs
beside a saucer of milk

Marguerite has
a bruised lemon to sell
and she'll show it to you
if you're perfectly still

how the snow
comes down
in Michigan
and I don't know
when I'm going to see you again
I think of the dog
in the passenger's seat
and I think of my mom

oh the snow
comes down
in Michigan
and I don't know
when I'm
going to see you again
I think of the dog
in the passenger's seat
and I think of my mom

I think of the dog
in the passenger's seat
and I think of my mom

Pennsylvania

hey Short Britches
have you got a porch for that swing?
I'm so lonely
you know I haven't been home since the spring

she says she loves me
but I know she wouldn't mind
if I never came home again

just keep the money
rolling in
baby just keep the money
rolling in

in Pennsylvania
you have to press your fingerprint
next to your signature
in order to cash a paycheque

I refused
I said I was allergic to the ink
I'll swell up　　I told the teller
my throat constricts — closes over until I can't
even whisper George Washington

but the teller wouldn't cash it
maybe you have some hypo-allergenic ink
I suggested
you know, I can't lick stamps either

latex is out of the question
but she wouldn't give in

I'm also allergic to beans   I said
and other legumes
shellfish, nuts, cats (but only when I eat them)
strawberries, chocolate, gasoline, leather shoes,
dandelion seeds, pantyhose (but only when I eat them)
mustard, dog food

all right   she said   *all right*
just give me two pieces of ID

when I left the bank
my pockets were fat with the heads
of presidents as obscure to me
as French kings

I didn't feel the least bit criminal
my hands were clean
and the lights were going to stay on
in Pennsylvania

still
living in the US
and working for the man
makes you
a conspiracy theorist

I know why they wanted that thumbprint
it was to authenticate the clone

they had started last spring in Montana
when they got my blood

a foreman came in with a tray of maple bars
and said
> *bad news*
> *you've all been exposed to lead*
> *blood tests after lunch*
> *have a maple bar*

and the guys were happy
free donuts

but I wouldn't give them my blood
not the red cells, not the white cells, the platelets
I'm using it all   I said
I have none for you

they got it anyhow
chased me around with a syringe
until I gave in

now there is a clone somewhere
waiting for a fingerprint so she can
read my poems
weld my tubes
cash my paycheques

my colleague, Tommy, is from South Carolina
he thinks I'm wrong about the clone
he says
> *oh no*   *they don't want any more of you*

they're always gambling here
cheque pool, pick a card, poker
raffle for a porcupine quill hatband
somebody made in prison

toy raffles for their kids' schools
and sports teams
and one day
gun raffle
get your tickets to the gun raffle
you could win shotguns, rifles
.22s for the kids, ammunition belts

are you raising money for your child's school?
I asked
        stupid Canadian!
        you can't have a gun raffle for a school
        and you can't enter anyhow — 'cause if you win
        they won't let you take the guns
        across the border

I thought if I won I'd donate them   *I said*
to the women's crisis centre next door to my hotel

these guns are only for huntin' Canadians
                              I was told.
oh no   Tommy said
it ain't no fun to hunt Canadians — they pacifists —
they don't wriggle around or nothin'

and mm mm mm

look at that handsome vest you can win

uh-huh, camouflage
it goes with anything

for some reason my frosty
Canadian union brothers
don't enjoy the boomers who come
up from the southern states
as much as I do

it's the accent   Dave said
I don't trust the way they talk

I thought of reminding him
that he is actually a guest
in their country, no matter how they talk
but instead I crossed the floor
and pinned my flag to a southerner's shirt
he said   *why thank-you, ma'am*
Cotton said
      she done tagged you now, boy

my countrymen were horrified
and the boy said *they lookin' at us*
         like we just swapped our chewin' gums
but I thought they'd like a little maple syrup
with their prejudice

they say
     a whipsnake

                      can charm birds
will crush its prey
                      in death coils
and will lash itself
                      out of your grasp
they say
      a wise collector of snakes
knows to take
            a good, firm, grip

somewhere   I mean
somewhere between the money and the guns
I tripped and stumbled

muscle became only muscle
breath became a threat
the joke about the sheet
strung up between the beds
became the rebel flag

I gambled away my tongue
in a game of Bourré
and I gave my eyes to the devil
because I knew he could use them

I gave my mind away
to North Carolina
to some southern boy who
threw flying squirrels high in the air
                just to see them
come down again

because he was
                      a dictionary of snakes

he had walked on the water moccasin
skinned the timber rattler
and slept with a copperhead
            in his pocket

and the heads of presidents
become crawfish
                    muscle becomes music
steel is rising water
and this smile

        is a truckstop

I am traveling

      south
                and west

anywhere

      away from this

                $25 hotel room

this rhapsody of scars

fill my head with tales of the bayou, baby
take me to the river

Judy, I Remembered

I remembered
the story I was
going to tell you

in the car
coming home
from the
tradeswomen's potluck

about
the pornography
how it doesn't
matter much
any more

in Grande Prairie
it was
the Victoria's Secret
centrefold
4 women
in matching
coloured bikini bras
and briefs

it's just 4 beautiful women
with beautiful bodies
                        he said
how can you
argue with that?

I found a photograph
in the *Edmonton Sun*
of a man
in a straw fedora
his pant legs
tucked in
to his high
rubber boots

they were tucked in
so the snakes
couldn't bite
his bare legs
or slide up
the dark cuffs
if they got loose

the picture was taken
because the man
had just broken
his own
Guinness Book
World Record
for holding
the most rattlesnakes
in his mouth
for the longest
period of time

his previous record
was 7 snakes

for 2 and a half minutes

this time
he had 12 snakes

                diamondbacks

he held them with their rattles
stuffed in his mouth
his hands held out
from his sides
like some crazy carnival Medusa
terrible and
                ridiculous

in the picture
the snakes
writhed around each
other, tangled up
hung down
past his knees and
poured from his mouth
as the crowd
counted
the seconds

56, 57, 58, 59,
                          4 minutes

                                      5 minutes

12 rattlesnakes

for 6 and a half minutes
or more
I don't remember
how long

I taped the photograph to the wall
in the lunchroom
next to the
Victoria's Secret girls
in their coloured
bikini briefs

and the guys
were grossed out

it's just a freaky old man
with a mouthful of snakes
                              I said
how can you
argue with that?

The Mouse
for Clint

we watched the sun go down
you and I
from level ten of the reactor tower
of the Esso refinery

you showed me
the photograph
of your girlfriend
                          Caroline
a big-busted aesthetician
in a tight white uniform
standing beside
an array of beauty products

for three weeks
you couldn't find
a single word
to say to me
didn't even look for one
and I crawled
over the tundra
of your language
slowly freezing
on that Acadian glacier

but in the fourth week
the foreman sent us
to the bottom

of Reactor #1
to weld out the last
of the scallop bar ring clips
and you had heard
that I had a tattoo
and you wanted
to see it

oh
you wanted to see it

the way any oversexed
Acadian boilermaker
alone in the bottom
of a tank with a woman
wants to see her tattoo
and I said *no*
the way any English girl
is expected
to say no

but I let you change my mind

I asked if you really
wanted to see it
and you said *yes*

it's a tattoo of a mouse
I said
here, on my hip
let me show you

and I unbuckled
my fall protection harness
and I unbuttoned
my coveralls
and shimmied them down
down in the bottom
of Reactor #1
and I pulled up layer
after layer
of turtleneck and T-shirt
and I undid my jeans
in that smoky wilderness
under the scaffold
and I pulled aside
my longjohns
and panties

I said   *there*
there   *do you see it?*

do you see the little mouse?

you looked and you said
                        I don't see it
I said   *look again*
and you looked and you looked
and you said

I still don't see it
there is nothing
there

so I looked, and I said

                                    shoot

my pussy must've eaten it

in my darkest times
I still see your laughing face
as we collapsed
against the bulkhead
in our sleep-starved hysteria
your brother had to pull us out
and we were unable
to tell him
the punchline
or why my pants
were down

later
outside the manway
you spoke to them in French
and the all-French crew
suddenly began
to speak English
and I learned
the French word
for mouse

on the final day
after the hatches
had been sealed
and the cables

had been loaded out
we were pressed together
against the screaming wind
sitting on the job-box
waiting for the layoff
looking at the photograph
         of Caroline

and you said

I love her
and I don't know why
she is with me
I don't know why

DICTIONARY
OF SNAKES

You Are Camping

you are camping
in the south
somewhere that is
semi-desert
that is hot   and dry
in the daytime
but that cools down
                cools right down
at night

you are camping and you wake up one morning
in your sleeping bag
and the sun is already blazing
over the horizon
the birds are awake
and it's a brand new day

but something is wrong

something is not quite right
you are lying   on your back
in your sleeping bag
you are lying
on your back
and something
is on your stomach

you feel a weight there
like a sleeping cat

like a sleeping lover's head
                but
it is not a cat
and it is definitely not a lover

what do you do when you
wake up in your sleeping bag
with a rattlesnake on your stomach?

you wonder if you are dreaming
but you do not stir yourself
because you know you are not dreaming
you think you must be mistaken
that this is not camping
there can be no snake
but you know you are not

mistaken

you panic
but suppress the urge to panic
before you move because panicking
will wake up and
potentially agitate
the snake

you lie very, very still
you deliberately relax your entire body
you take slow, deep breaths
you think of the people you love
and the people who love you

you think of solutions

you think about very, very
carefully unzipping
your sleeping bag and opening it up
but you don't do this
because it will wake up
and potentially agitate the snake

you think of a time bomb
you think of anesthesia
you try to remember
what you are supposed to do if this ever happens to you

you try to remember the cure
for snakebite

Oh, My Dear

oh, my dear
I have just been bitten
by a poisonous snake
and I want to tell you
that I am not afraid of death
I have been preparing for this
my entire life

since I was four
and my brother and I
would draw two dots on each other's arms
and pretend they were the marks
left from the fangs of rattlesnakes

we would take turns biting each other's arms
and sucking on the dots
until the ink turned our teeth blue
then we would spit
and spit out
the imaginary venom

we wrapped each other's arms
in strips of flannelette from old, torn-up pajamas
I would tie my strips as tight as I could
but I was four
     and he was eight
he would tie his tighter and tighter and tighter
until my fingers turned blue

then he would look very serious and say
>	*I couldn't get all the venom.*
>	*I tried, but I couldn't get it*

He would have mud on his face for camouflage
from whatever adventure we had been on – army maneuvers
or Lawrence of Arabia
>		or Maxwell Smart

he would look very sombre and say
>	*you're going to die*

and for a moment
my four-year-old heart would skip
giddy with the thought
of my impending death
>	*it's too soon*
I'd say
>	*I'm not ready*

he would make me act out the symptoms of snakebite
the fever
the delirium
similar to malaria
but with a lot of yelling
and in the final stages
I had to lie very, very still
not even breathing

>		*it's no good*
he'd say

pulling out his pocket knife
      I have to operate
arguments followed
about whether you could use a real knife
to cut open a pretend snakebite
whether you were allowed
to draw real blood

   wait   I would yell
as he tried to stab me
      I think I'm getting better!

oh, my dear
I do not know if this snakebite is real
or if I dreamed it
if it was an accident
or if I deserved it
and I want to tell you
that I am not afraid of death

The Letter

dear Mr. Riversnake
you are a looker
you have that certain something
that certain
        something
I forget what it's called

dear Mr. Riversnake
if you were a dog
I would say
what a great dog this is
take a look at this dog
I could play with this dog all day
I could play with this dog
I could play
with this dog
all day long

but you are not my dog
you are somebody else's dog
I already have
a dog at home
he doesn't like other dogs
that much

dear Mr. Riversnake
if you were a man
I would say that
you are very sweet

very charming
oh you are very sleek
and leathery
that you are
leathery
that you are

Mr. Riversnake
I am sure that there are lots of girls
who have wanted to take you home
who have wanted to take you home with them
over the years
but you wouldn't fit in
you wouldn't fit in around here

but you do remind me of a man
a lonely man
an obedient man

you remind me of a dog
a not very smart dog
what is out of sight
is completely out of mind
you stray beyond whistling distance
and forget what's left behind

you have terrible
table manners
but a tremendous appetite
no concern for anyone else
so long as you're all right

oh that you are

yes you are so
undomesticated
so poisonous, untamed, yes
that you are
                    poisonous
that you are
untamed   yes

irresistible, Mr. Riversnake
you are a cold-blooded animal, yes
an absolute reptile, yes
you would not fit in,
yes
and if you were,
yes
and if you were
yes

Mr. Riversnake
you are a looker

Esmeralda
(a ballad in two parts)

i.

it was a terrible day for a drive
with the rain coming on
we headed outside
and there was nothing to do
nothing to say
except how are things

this road is the chorus to the song
broken and rough
and a little too winding
I'm sorry if what I said was wrong
if I laughed too loud
or waited too long

old, married man
what do you think that I am?
doctor oh doctor
get here as quick as you can
'cause that snake in the grass
has got me again

ii.

oh Esmeralda
I see you
I see your heart
when it opens wide
I see the snakes come

in all around you
can we get to you in time?

oh Esmeralda
you may be poisoned
you may be gone
to the other side
think of your true love
think of your boys then
and return to us tonight

oh my true love
I have been poisoned
and I have seen the snake
the has bitten me
but do not grieve, love
for I have killed him
and that snake I saw
was thee

THESE
TANGLED
MUSTANGS

The Last Frontier

the last frontier
        is this hotel room
you are riding a black horse
        and I am tracking you

with only desert and sagebrush and snakes to get through
you better sit down on the edge of that bed and do nothing

your smile is the final smile
it reminds me of the guy
who was driving the hearse
the one who locked his keys inside
        when he was
trying to leave the church and it was a hot day
        in the desert
                it's a hot day for dying
you think I'm your prisoner
and I think you're mine

you better sit down on the edge
of that bed and do nothing

from behind this rock
I see you climb that ridge
I'd be right on your tail
but you've burned that bridge
you're out of luck
        and I'm out of room

and we've run out
of things to talk about
you'll be leaving soon

you better sit
down
on the edge
of that bed
and do
nothing

Miles City

the sign reminds you
to cast your ballot
it's hanging in the window
of the barbed-wire museum

they're electing a coroner
in Rosebud County
and the way things are going
you know we're going to need him

hang your head
hold your hardened heart
as you cross the Tongue River
to sell your guitar

I'll see your tattoo
I'll raise you a scar
don't you think that
she'll come around?

it's only a gun
I'm only a river
in this indigo wind
this starry apartment

so hold your black tongue
hang onto your heart
don't you think that
she'll come around?

it's only a gun
I'm only a river
don't you think that
she'll come around?

Cowboys Dream
(score for two voices)

Cowboys dream
of the open plains
of the tumbleweeds
and the golden grains

it's been three weeks

that

you've been
away

your horse is restless
and your dogs are howling

your horse
is restless

your dogs
are howling

                                        when I think of you
                                        on those open plains
                                        it is always at night
                                        and
                                        I am riding
                                        barefoot

in front of me
the pricked up ears
of the bay horse
tremble to the call
of the tall grass
the song of the long grass
the sound of open ground

locked onto the horizon
the black spiders
the oil rigs
heaving
                       dinosaurs
that split the silence

we thread between the dead
following
the promise of gold

I think of Jane
asleep somewhere
underneath that racket

or else wide awake
and hard at it
halogen illuminated

repairing infrastructure
joining steel to steel
and standing on her own handiwork
15 storeys above the prairie

        the sun will beat you down
        to eat
        to sleep away the day
        in a narrow bed
        in an empty barracks

cowboys play
at home on the range
at night they say
how rich and strange

have been these days
this pony's life

Over this mountain
I hear there's prairie
I hear there's open ground

they say
you aren't anybody
until you're someone
I wish you were someone else
I wish you were yourself.

Oh my sweet little cowboy
how could I
ever feel sorry for you
you say you're angry
because the oilman
has stolen your prairie
but in the end you'll work for him

    because you're just as bad

                      I dream of Jane
                      and of
                      birdsong and thunder

                      of the night sky
                      the burning fields
                      and my own hand
                      on the smooth seat
                      of an old saddle

history teaches us
make no mistake
it's your fault
if you're late

fever comforts
like a dry spring
            delirious
open meadow
I wait for you
and you're late

somewhere
there's a distance
can be traveled
can be flown through

broken meadow

delirious

I wait for you
and you're late

I'm not sorry
for the things I've said
or for the things you do

like lighting up the sky
over the forest
        the rest of the storm
enters the house before us.

        when you are setting out to
        catch a wild horse
        do not try to grab him by the foot
        put your arms around his neck
        stand strong
        remember past obediences

        each night
        when she closes her eyes
        she sees them
                      conjured from a forest
        backed into the trees
        heads low
        or bunched up
        in a howling wind
        dusted lightly with snow

        what are they trying to tell her?

these tangled mustangs
these wild ghosts
they're saying

watch the trail
brave the winter
wait for new shoots
don't be seduced by a handful of coarse hay
don't let them slip that smooth new rope
around your tangled mane

Buffalo

do you remember the day that the buffaloes
flew through the air?
the babies stayed close to their mothers
and the mothers couldn't believe it
they just kept on falling

their thunder kept rolling
and so did the movie

the camera caught everything
even John Wayne at the edge of the cliff
looking down through the dust
at that pile of bodies
and when the air clears
you see he's dressed like an indian

hollywood indian
broken buffalo
saturday matinee
big money maker

I want to turn back the clock
roll back the film
see him take off his make up
see the buffaloes go up, up, up

but you can't go back
not for all that you've got
not for all the pictures you steal

not for all the dollars in hollywood
no you can't bring them back
not for all the sticks that you pick up
not for all the lies that you make up
not for all the dust that you kick up

not for all the nights that you crack up
not for all the cars that you smash up
not for all the toasts that you drink up
not for all the ghosts that you bring up

oooo-oo oooo-ooooo ooo-oooooo
(i don't want to be in your movie)

Outlaw Girls

Honey hit the open road
with her gun still smoking
Honey was an outlaw
she was a wanted poster
she was a photograph
on every lamppost
in her eyes

Honey was an outlaw
she had no time for anything
she was a churlish thing
with a girlish disposition

they say she was too emotional
they say that it was all hormonal
and today they can treat these things
they say that she was moody
but she was only mad
and they say
that she was crazy
(they say
that she was crazy)
but she was only mad

the night Honey pulled into town
she looked like a wildcat
she'd been driving all night
through a craziness
that left her ragged and torn-up

she was escaping the remains
of a nasty little love affair
just driving the backroads from town to
town with her memories devouring her
mind's eye like locusts and her heart so
near to breaking that every cloud or
tumbleweed or lone coyote caused her
to gasp and stumble and her own tired
lonely spirit was forcing her over to the
side of the road

the night Honey pulled into town
all she saw was one more nameless ugly
little smalltown barroom full
of nameless ugly little cowpokes soaking
their daily fears and longings in big glasses
of watery beer

she ordered two shots
and drank them
without breaking eye contact
with the bartender
who was later heard to remark

> it was as though i had locked eyes
> with something
> completely wild
> something i have never
> locked eyes with
> before

Billy was ten times meaner
than any alleycat
and not nearly so handsome

he spent his spare time brooding
dodging bullets
and thinking up new ways to die
he was on his 28th beer
and couldn't get drunk
he'd spent the day shooting the heads
off dandelions with a singleshot .22
and now he was waiting for night to fall
so he could go driving

when he saw Honey
something broke inside
and he had to ask her
> *are you waiting*
> *for somebody?*

Honey had a mean streak
that ran clean through her
and she was in no mood
she said
> *I'm in no mood*

Billy leveled his buckshot eyes and said
> *because if you're not waiting*
> *I thought maybe*

and that was the first night
they locked antlers

the first
of thirteen solid days and nights
of lawlessness
they drove out along an abandoned
dirt road with a bottle between them
just before the railroad bridge
Billy stopped the truck
and pulled out his bow

they attached sticks of dynamite
to the arrows, lit them and
fired them across the river
in sparkling arcs
that sent up sudden
feathery explosions
of sand and water
on the opposite shore

Honey smelled like a cloudy day
and dragged Billy across the desert
he buried her in wildflowers
she snapped him
a dream on a line
he fired her like a pistol
and she read him like a sermon

they were a herd of buffaloes
stampeding over a mountain
a sky full of black clouds
and they were criminal

they were behaving like hound dogs
they fucked like alleycats
like rabbits and then like elk
(Honey kicked him square with her split hoof)
like timber falling
out of the sky
like a tsunami
or a particular
frail moonrise

they fucked like a housefire
the flames screaming up
from the inside out
like a snowstorm
billowing huge banks of snow
against the riverbank
then quiet and solemn
as the inside of a chapel at dusk

when it was over
when the sun was
throwing its saddle
over the horizon

Billy lay still

Honey shook herself down
like a wet dog getting out
of the pond and she saw
they were two
of the same brand

the next day
they packed up
and toured the land
they ate only in diners
shaped like
gigantic food
lived on Gourmet Burgers
Homemade Pies
and coffee drunk from overthick cups

they filled the glovebox with snackfoods
named after baseball players
collected pens that had things in them
that slid from one end to the other
listened to cassette tapes
lifted from gas stations and sought out
long forgotten roadside attractions
and asked strangers
to take their photographs

when they were too tired to sleep
they pulled into the nearest motel
and fucked on the foldout bed
and only used novelty condoms
that always broke

for thirteen days
they slammed arrows into nightmares
committed small political acts
with short-fused explosives
stampeded in rainwater

rolled in honeysuckles and undid
their own misgivings

and on the thirteenth night
Honey woke up on a hotel roof
with all the blankets from all the rooms
of the fourth floor piled up around her
and all the constellations reflected
against Billy's shimmery side

she looked at Billy then
sleeping all covered
in hornets and sorrow
and she realized for the first time
that she had tied herself
to a crazyman
she had tied herself to a man
who was a river

but worse than this
she had tied herself up
to a runaway train
she had tied herself
inside herself
she had
tied herself
inside herself

thirteen days of landbased adventures
and now she was slipping him
her honeylaquered absence

she was restless
she could hear the truck
stomping at the side of the road
and it was too much
the way Billy had started looking at her
as though she had just
walked out of a storm

all the nights
stretched behind her
like the broken ties
of a railway line

she was caught in time
she was blinded
she was hungry
and angry

O Honey

she picked up her gun
and reached for
her clothing
she put it on
she reached
down in the pocket deep
down in the pocket
for that handful of bullets
and she pulled out one

and she loaded her gun

O Honey

Honey bent down
over that sleeping outlaw
and her lips were gun-barrel cool
she pressed them against the ear
of that crazy river and she said

> *i will love you*
> *over and over*
>
> *i will love you*
> *over and over*
> *and over and over again*
> *and again*

and she loaded her gun

> *i will love you*
> *over and over*
> *and over and over*
>   *again*
> *again*
> *and again and again*
>
> again and
> again and again
>
> and she was gone
>   she was gone
> gone

Honey hit the open road
with her gun still smoking
and that blackeyed devil
still hung inside her
that Billy still hung in her
eyes like a star

she drove into the underwoods
a traveler of dreams
chasing the mountains
where the catroads and dirttracks
snaked through the slash like a
handrawn map of all her veins and arteries

and when she ran out of road
she drove straight through the alders
keeping it slow and even
remembering her way from centuries before

and when she could drive no further
Honey got out and walked
deep into the underbrush through
salal and huckleberry
she climbed all the way up
then down and down
through the razorgrass and skunkcabbage
dropping down into
the pocket of the mountain
that held the most sacred dreaming

there was a stream
that turned a corner perfectly
cutting deep and shady trout hideouts
into the riverbank
there was a fork in that stream
and at this crossing there was a pool

Honey could see
the brooktrout there
cutting lazy figure eights
against the gravelbed
circling and conniving
in its roughshod consciousness
she could see her own reflection
over the surface of the pool
her image intermittently broken
by descending midges
and dragonflies

and as she leaned back
and gazed into the mountain
an image wound its way
into Honey's vision
the way a brooktrout
will flash its scaly side
slowly back and forth
under the pondwater

in the vision she saw Billy
with whom she had
committed glorious crimes

he was laughing
and he was tangled up
he was all tied up
with the law
the pretty bartender
and the promises he'd never keep
he was tangled in the barbed wire
of his own lies and conniving
and a life so far from grace
he could only fall
and laugh
and fall

in the dream
he was laughing
and falling

Billy was as crooked
as a snake in a cactus patch
and Honey wasn't having
her haunches spurred
by any rustler

but before she could be overcome
by the icy shadow of this grave insight
a second vision came sidling up
came sliding through the afterwaters
of the first and Honey started to see shapes
just under the pondwater and these shapes
changed and collided there in the trout pond
until she could make out what they were

and what they were

they were other outlaw girls
thousands of others and some
carried guns and some
carried irises or sandwiches
and some carried children
on their backs and walked
with their empty hands held out

they drove pick-up trucks
bicycles and horses
and rode buses and ran
wore ice skates
drove backhoes
and rode elevators all the way up,

                                                up

they worked in factories
and offices and bakeries and
prisons and research stations
hospitals and schools
electrical plants, pulp mills
and political organizations

the truth flashed its
scaly brooktrout skin
that day under the shining water
and now lay gasping
in the open its silver gills

choking and its scaly sides
shining on the surface of
that sunlit afternoon

Honey climbed out
and saddled up her own
lonesome soul
and deepdrawn hunger
and when she lit out
on the highway that day
her hair restless with salal
her skin streaked with
screaming amanitas
she couldn't stop thinking
about all the outlaw girls
streaked in saltwater and honeyblossoms

and as she drove
along that gravelly road
she started seeing them everywhere
rolling naked
over the heartland